Hunter Johnson Presents…

Runt of the Litter: Prayers of a Po' Boy

DEDICATION

To God be the glory. This project is dedicated to my beloved Lanett, AL—
the city that loved and supported me; challenged me to strive for big things
while staying rooted. I love you all. I will continue to try to make you
proud.

CONTENTS

Dance With Who Brought You

Hope Dealer

I'm doing what I do, with seemless worries and without a care;
As of yet, never flew the friendly skies, but I have a regal air.
Success was so attractive, I could not resist and had to flirt with;
I flipped it and I twerked it, made the worthless seem so worth it.

I was always glad as a poor lad, and consider it my testing;
You never miss what you've never had, so consider surplus a blessing.
Gumption is the referee to mediate it;
Opportunity's not granted to all, so I really appreciate it.

There is nothing wrong, with reaching out for help,
Just as long as you are trying, and willing to help yourself.
A way, you've gotta try and find; these, they are trying times;
Just truth, there are no lies in mine; I do not have a crying dime.

I ask no one for nothing, yet, they are wishing to give it;
I guess it is a testament, to the way that I've been living.
Even in uncertain times, not mistaken for a miser;
Maybe not long live the king, but, surely, long ride for Survivor.

Bull Market

Values are dropping, so the economy is failing;
Quality is hard to find, so our society's ailing.
Reaching for the end of the bench, to put the last ones first,
Preaching that it's not always the price, that's determinant of worth.

Always shopping around, to find best for least cost,
And taking minimal gains, sometimes, just to offset the loss.
Doing away with trends of now, to better replace them with class,
Investing in livestock for the future, getting rid of bull from the past.

If you listen closely, you will see what I confront;
In the passing of this passage, I have not mentioned money, once.
Not once, you say, I've been deceived by my very eyes;
I have just helped you to see, where your true value lies.

Fan of Man

There is so much calamity,
Such stirring and so much fuss.
Leaving us faced with two decisions:
Either rise and speak or sit and hush.

Most folks would say there's no saving the world,
So there is no use in trying.
Personally, I say I can do my part,
To leave it better than I find it.

What could that mean—help fulfill dreams,
Give a dollar to someone who needs lending.
Or it might not cost one red cent,
Just lend an ear to someone needing befriending.

Whether the drunk grouch in the gutter,
Or CEO in his luxury home.
The world's a huge place to live in;
And no one should have to be here, alone.

When my time has come and gone,
And will never come, again.
I would hope that it could be said,
That Mankind has lost its friend.

It's apparent we inherited life;
This world was given and prearranged.
Maybe it's idealistic of me to think,
That everything can change.

Benevolence to brethren should be evident;
And compassion shown whenever it can.
Some may say I'm a silly fool;
I say that I am a fan of man.

Good Input

Upfront leaves not reasons to confront—
No need to make amends.
Honesty causes mention, honorably;
While secrets will only cost one friends.

Public praise and admiration,
Can cause a vicious vice to loosen.
While Twit posts and Post-It notes,
May just result in confusion.

I've learned when to speak,
And when to silence myself.
That there's a time to fight,
And when to alliance myself.

That life can be a battle,
Of which you can learn to thrive in.
And people become ornery as cattle,
If you push them away and always drive them.

That you'll become more adept to beef if,
With it, you become a chef.
But if you continue to serve it up,
You'll be, more than less, by yourself.

Best practice, in regard to positivity,
Is, simply, to do it.
Don't concentrate so much on taking bad from the world,
Instead, putting good into it.

Ladened Traveler

I think that it is about time,
That you took time to learn a lesson.
So pull yourself up a chair,
Because class is, now, in session.

So many times, in history,
Time's sands have been marked by movements.
Provoked by disrupting status quo—
Readied for renaissance through revolution.

In my mind, I conclude,
That if we are to come together.
We need a new-age revolution,
And we need it more than ever.

One of widespread brotherhood,
Far above pettiness of cliques and factions.
Never dormant in duplicity,
Nor on educational ration.

Instead, a resting place and haven,
That is socially respondent.
With basic benevolence in her bosom,
And universal love in abundance.

Where faith is always fashionable,
Good deeds for sake of doing are doubled.
So the weary and ladened traveler,
Can get away from his heavy troubles.

I wait and pray to see that day,
When our world will finally make up.
"Us" and "we" will replace "them" and "they,"
Whenever we are ready to wake up.

I may not see the end result,
But my lineage will see the progress.
It is my prayer that they will do best,
To help speed along the process.

Leaders and the Lead

Before you ever enter into battle,
Or can have the hope to contend or win.
It's important that you understand,
Who can motivate the hearts of men.

Here, we're discussing those that can stir embers,
Inside of a man's soul.
Also, those that become dead weight to forward progress,
Like lead lumps or pieces of coal.

Just so it's understood as intended,
I will provide some clarity.
But I'll say it how I mean it—
I could care less about popularity.

The goal should be,
To learn how to make less more.
Though you may never ever be the best,
A leader can make those around them better.

But if you were not meant to lead,
If this isn't the cloth from which you are cut.
So be it, but there is no need,
For you to make bad matters worse.

Lonely Finish Line

If you were ever hungry and,
Now, know what it's like to win.
Vow, to yourself,
You won't ever be there, again.

If you know about the scraps and crumbs,
It can be done but is no fun.
Fret not; press on 'til you see the light;
Night is darkest before morning comes.

Each day you rise, keep hope alive;
Pledge to live your dreams.
Have a made up mind for hunger to cease and desist;
Feast on meals fit for kings.

The process of pressing diamonds may,
In itself, prove to be pain-staking.
But, trust that strength in hardships,
Is wisdom in the making.

When you're hungry for being better,
Your appetite should never fill.
Passion is like thirst;
It pushes and grabs at you until you are filled.

Allow determination to be a force of your heart,
That is always ripping through.
If anyone says you'll never be somebody,
They're nobody for you to listen to.

Don't let the illusion of despair,
Get you tricked and have you fooled.
You had better accept that life's not fair;
Then, make up and live by your own rules.

Make a declaration,
To get the lint out of your pocket.
Replaced with coins in your coffer,
And crisp dollars in your wallet.

Plan your work and work your plan;
Your plans will surely pan out.
Falling down's presented to all,
But those that refuse are the ones who stand out.

Fanning flames are ignited,
From the likes of a single spark.
Losing is no option to winners,
And if you think you are, you are.

When you're willing to put in work,
And also invest the time.
Striving and hitting the mark,
Always justifies the grind.

Ever wonder why you see no one,
While you are out on the grind?
The race is crowded by those that won't push,
To the lonely finish line.

Make up in your mind to make a change;
Don't just sit around and pout.
Because you never saw a homerun hit,
By someone who was afraid to strike out.

Leave small things for small thinkers;
There are enough of them by the score.
Refuse to lie down and take what's given;
Instead, rise to take what's yours.

Make it Truth

Though I had a subtle walk,
It was respect I demanded I would be getting.
Never a daddy, by far,
Didn't need a strap to make them listen.

Sometimes, resistance, to progress is limited,
When there's help through the door.
No one can keep their eyes on the prize,
Without an idea of what they're working for.

It's proven the knowledge of the past,
Can be the youth's best protection.
Because it's understood anyone can make a wrong turn,
When they lack direction.

Teach them to face life head on,
Even when they can't tell right from left.
Rest when needed, retreat if need be,
Move forth if opportunity presents itself.

A lot of people talk about saving the world,
Making claims of what they do.
But all talking is lies,
Unless there's action behind it to make it truth.

Kill Yourself

Now, don't take this literally, and knock off your own block;
Take the time, to open your mind, and think outside the box.
Don't go suck on a pistol, in order to loosen the back of your braids,
Or hit the dirty needle, to catch a quick case of the AIDS.

I'm not suggesting you get in the pool,
And refuse to hold your breath.
But, my friend, I do advise,
That you go and kill yourself.

(Here's how...)

Be brave in your deeds, and steadfastly courageous;
To honor, be cleaved—dogmatically tenacious.
Set missions and objectives, and obtainable goals;
Offset misfortunes, and sidestep potholes.

As a striding greyhound,
You must pursue the rabbit.
And when you run it down,
You better jump up and grab it.

Leave the suicide letters in a movie in frail nights,
The poison in the mouse traps, carbon monoxide in tailpipes.
Don't sit in the bathtub and open up your red veins,
Refrain from any actions that could result in your pain.

This is the flat truth,
And as quiet is kept.
There is but one option,
And that is to kill yourself.

(Secret is...)

Risk it and pull on the rope 'til you make it;
Nothing is given in life; you've gotta get down and take it.
Don't sing to the beat or ,like a jig, up and dance;
Be the maestro; don't just play in the band.

Become the next legend; let memories ever-survive;
Move from dying to live into living to die.

Full Steam Ahead

In the process, as you progress to the next success,
It's important that you not let, yourself regress into the stress of the cess.
Vow that you will have the best—nothing more and nothing less;
And know that anything less, would just prove to be a mess.

I think about the top, and I dream about it, often;
Trust and believe, ambition is something I'll never come up short in.
All that matters, now, is the battle before me, now—
No thoughts of yesterday's fights or tomorrow's title bouts.

No need for life long-gone, to make me live, lividly;
Instead, living vivacious and vivid, gives my life license and validity.
Thankful for what I have, not what I've had or what I'll get;
Hyper-focused on the gifted present, enjoy it, now, why, I insist.

Longevity vs. Brevity

What does she do when the jazzy girl,
Is no longer paid for looks?
Or when ballers become of the boys,
Once laughed at for their love for books?

Or when beauty queens lose their looks,
And no one yearns to toot their butts up?
And dope boys get popped by Johnny Law,
And can no longer pay for cut-up?

Where do church folks go for gossip,
When their cohorts begin to dismiss them?
And how do they make up their lost time,
And get long-term faith of a Christian?

How do the "haves" fight guilt,
When the "have nots" make them see the.
True purpose, in life, when they take their little,
And still try to feed the needy?

How does the young girl feel, as she grows up,
And realizes Mama didn't wanna hurt her?
The only reason she was so strict,
Was to instill value for virtue to be nurtured?

Or the young boy who grows into a man,
And sees that Daddy chastised and didn't praise him.
Just so he could teach him well,
So the law would not have to raise him?

Present and
Accounted For

I'm not sure how well you slept—
If you tossed and turned or snored.
But if someone were to call your name,
You could answer, "Present and accounted for."

You may have woke up with aches and pains,
Without one nickel or dime.
Judging by the fact you're reading this,
You're breathing and, thus, alive.

The light bill might've hit you;
And your sight doesn't let you see clear.
Your lover might've quit you;
But it's a blessing just to be here.

The blues may be all that you hear;
Messy divorce has helped split up your home.
In spite of all the bad,
You're still here instead of dead and gone.

You're blessed not to have to be dressed on a table—
Prepared for going into the ground.
Be thankful for that fact,
Instead of bringing down those all around.

I'm just shedding light on the issue;
Because I feel it's really needed.
Far from perfect, so I'm not judging;
I'm just calling it like I see it.

Stop feeling sorry for yourself;
Quit trying to find escape.
Step away from the pipe or syringe;
Give the liquor bottle a break.

Or keep wallowing in sorrow,
Wanting death instead of dealing with it.
But please be careful what you ask for;
Because there's a chance that you will get it.

The Learning Process

My money is low, and I'm flunking my classes;
And if that ain't enough, the doctor says I need glasses.
Life issues its blows, to my trunk like a pugilist;
Anybody else would say, "the hell," and be through with it.

Death in my circle, a devastation to my nation,
Green backs are so slow, it's not just a revelation.
Sight's getting blurry, but my vision won't falter,
Just pack them up in me, and take them to the altar.

Some people would give up, before they'd even try;
I just look to the sky and call the devil a lie.
This subject always troubles me, and I often wonder why;
Everyone wants to see Heaven, but don't nobody wanna die.

You have to see a frown in order for a smile to mean enough,
Just like you have to be knocked down, before you learn to get up.

Bye and Bye

The plan I set forth for myself has,
So far, proved to be alright.
Like John Boy Walton, I bid farewell to all,
Before I decide to call it a night.

Might not get to everyone,
But Lord knows I try.
I know nothing is guaranteed;
And this might be the last good bye.

Let me rephrase what I already said;
I say good bye next to never.
Mama T taught me to say "I'll see you later,"
'Cause good bye means you're gone forever.

I speak to each and every passerby, or wish that I should have done;
And before we part in ways, I wish that they have a good one.
Call me a teddy bear at heart, or sensitive in my senses,
But when I say to have a good day, you'd best believe I meant it.

When it comes to encounters, like pleasantries and such,
Speaking is essential, but closing encounters mean as much.

Due Dilligence

The world, today, has many, seemingly, losing control,
Like the devil's make-shifting morality, and he's shoplifting their soul.
Some try to turn blind eyes to how, evil exists and is constantly happening;
Crime has not taken a break, and carjackers are steadily window-tapping.

I've been patiently waiting on faith—constantly clocking countless hours,
Not willing to pawn my soul, for a quicker seat of power.
When you're tested by the trials of life, doing right may yield the hardest;
So I invest in high volumes in sowing, to reap high volumes in the harvest.

Never took proposition for complete evil, though, I've certainly had one,
When prayers go up, blessings come down—no arguing with that one.
Concentrate on putting the good in, instead of taking the hell out;
Understand that, first, you must buy in, before you can ever sell out.

Please purge your urge and cleanse on it;
Approach due diligence, like your life depends on it.
Spend less time preaching at folks and invest time in living it and praying;
To really get the people going, tell them it's what the streets are saying.

Eyes and Ears of the Streets

Crime is on the rise, and unemployment ain't no joke;
Looks like gray clouds won't ever move, and we're quickly losing hope.
Seems like taxes are going up, and paychecks are going down;
Smiles of yesterday are replaced, today, by frowns.

Drugs still come like rain in floods; crooks steal anything they can;
Few try to lend a hand, in order to help their fellow man.
But make no mistake, that's what is but doesn't have to be;
We can change the world, if we just open our eyes to see.

Let's help save our communities—be the eyes and ears of the streets,
Care less of "snitching," and help protect and serve with the police.

Betwixt and Between

My mind was on a battlefield,
Betwixt and between the fight.
A devil was on my left lapel;
A heavenly sprite was on my right.

I took a better look,
And wanted more than usual trickiness.
This feeling seemed to be,
What would ween me away from the wickedness.

Hopefully, I can offer some help,
Or maybe help prevent something.
Do something worthwhile in life,
So when it ends, folks'll say my life meant something.

Say a word that will motivate, making someone press even harder,
Or be a type of surrogate, a stand-in for someone who needs a father.
Being more than one whispering sweet nothings, making hearts melt,
Trying to scratch names on the bed post, and add notches to my belt.

Successful in staying calm, a pleasant alternative to rage,
A servant to the King of Kings, a fulfilled calling in this present age.

Driving the Heard

I always wanted to be top dog; best view goes to head of the pack;
Only way to lead's out front; you can only drive from the back.
Goals should be what push you; there's nothing to scoff and smirk at;
If for no other reason but this, they give you something to work at.

Striving hard and hitting the mark, seems to justify the grind,
Sharing glory with the hands that helped, gives all opportunity to shine.
Being the man around town, will surely get you hugged and kissed;
Getting relaxation and a bit of rest, is rejuvenating as hard work is.

And when you finally make it, don't become too much or get offended;
If someone asks a favor, if you've got it, try to lend it.
Practice patience while waiting on what's for you; don't be an eager beaver;
And always try and keep the attitude, that you wanna be a servant leader.

Band of Brothers

The dawn of a new day, the rainbow after the rain,
We are upon a new day, the eve of needed change.
Times gradually changing, from where our forefathers brought us,
Technology ever-evolving, from what the cave men taught us.

All races live together, embracing one another,
Love shielding the weather—finally, a band of brothers.
Positives of the present, trumping negatives of the past,
And vision for the future, ensures that change we've found will last.

Absence vs. Lack of Presence

The issue of absence doesn't equate the lack of presence;
I will not be the one to refute this.
I feel anyone who believes any different,
Is helping to perpetuate useless excuses.

That's like saying if my mom wouldn't work,
I'd be more inclined to quit.
Or if my dad were absent, then,
I'd be less likely to amount to shit.

Or if a different man each night,
Were the road a mother chose.
Her daughter would find a profession of hooking,
Or dropping down the pole.

True, environment may play a part,
In molding overall attitudes.
But we'd be remiss to think the deciding factor,
Isn't our personal fortitude.

Things of our past, deserve their due homage and their deference,
But absence, in its harshest form, is no excuse for a lack of presence.

Smiling Faces

The light bill's late; rent is due by next week;
And I couldn't be happier, smiling at life as we speak.
Life's full of peril and turmoil, tribulations and trials;
But it is what you make it, with each and every frown's denial.

Of all of the anger and malice, things to make you bitter,
Make you wipe your hands of it all, or let you consider a quitter.
Happiness is peace within the life you live,
Gratified from within, the gifts you give.

The grins inside a sea of frowns,
Manifested ups in life's great downs.
Why waste your time; instead, enjoy every day;
Live life in the present, and come what will or may.

Night Man

As I worked the graveyard shift,
The rain pounded on my head.
While others slumbered and they slept—
Were comforted in their beds.

I thought of ways to simplify things,
So people would always understand me.
How to help others better help themselves—
Ways to provide for my family.

So hell-bent on becoming better, and readying relief,
That I oppress my needs, and am willing to miss out on sleep.
The mark was already set for me; it's obligation that I hit it;
It's declarative that I want it, but it's imperative that I get it.

Like a no-look pass in the lane, it's unexpected but, still, connected;
Like a shot pinned to the glass, can be rejected if they don't respect it.
There have been low groceries, too long—gonna make sure we eat;
To hell with noodles and bologna; now, I want potatoes and meat.

Hallelujah Anyhow

Violence is on every horizon;
Right is keeping quiet while wrong continues to riot.
Paychecks are growing puny,
And the meals on plates, seemingly, are on diets.

Signs of the times are everywhere;
Last days' warnings are showing, now.
But even with this plight in sight,
I say, "Hallelujah, anyhow."

Focus is quickly fleeting, and will power is on the wane;
Gain's remaining hard to come by, but pain still stays the same.
But faith is what lets us press on, when we know not why or how;
It's in those times that we must just say, "Hallelujah, anyhow."

The world is so accepting and even intrigued and engulfed with sin;
It's hard to discern where it ends and where true right begins.
But even as it seems that there is wickedness all around,
We have to look evil in the eye and scream, "Hallelujah, anyhow."

The big man bullies the little guy—through muscle, imposes his will,
Taking as much as he sees fit, seldom earning it with work and skill.
The rich grow in stature, while pushing the poor into the ground;
Even in iniquity, righteousness equalizes, so "Hallelujah, anyhow."

Love Shown Because of Love Felt

I grew up and went to school, with some people so rarely happy;
Dressed in best and groomed up nicely, but attitudes were very nasty.
Their clothes were nice; I'd find my mind being so off put;
What I'd find but wondered why, their minds didn't match looks.

Now, that I am older, I understand what I only got, in part;
I've learned to do what God does, and inventory the heart.
Those same kids sitting beside me, who had but acted in bad fashion,
Were those for whom I began, to feel the most compassion.

Most of them had providing parents, who didn't give kisses and hugs;
And through all of the material things, they lacked owning love.
It was something foreign, and so far-fetched for me to imagine;
Because of love that I was shown, I knew not what had happened.

I never felt neglected; Mama hugged and held me when I wept;
Ever was I protected, Daddy peeped in to check on me while I slept.
Some things I didn't get as a child; wants, I got some of them;
If I had to account for anything I lacked, love wasn't one of them.

Nothing Outdo You

It was a morsel of wisdom, being passed from past to the future;
My daddy told me his daddy told him "not to let nothing outdo you."
This isn't strange; it was straightforward and in no way less than that;
Regardless of what I faced, I should not, with it, be bested at.

Never should I have a reason, to leave feeling defeated;
Because any obstacle in my path, I should find a way to beat it.
True, you must lose as well as win, as part of playing the game;
But if you give your best to find a way, fulfillment should remain.

There will be times we come up short; that I can deal with;
But having given all that I had to give, makes it easier to live with.
No matter if it's a recipe or study or stubborn kitchen sink,
My daddy's daddy told my daddy to not be outdone by anything.

Charge of Credit

Steer clear of it; don't go anywhere around it;
If you ever come close, you'd better leave it where you found it.
People I know have been bound down and, now, are sounding,
Like water is all-surrounding, and they are in danger of drowning.

He always used cash—long before cards came for a debit;
Daddy taught me that credit is a load that gets heavy if you let it.
Your funds could dwindle, just like the wax of a candle;
Interest will add more to your plate, than your wallet can handle.

What a valuable lesson, learned from the age of his days,
Watching my daddy avoid credit, like its wage were the plague.
There's no need in fronting; my daddy really taught me something;
Either work and save for what you want, or else keep on wanting.

The Color of Money

I'm sure, as I say this, you say, "What does he mean;
Any fool with eyes can see, that the color of money is green."
I do respect your opinion, but will have to beg to differ;
The color of money depends on the community it exits and enters.

As a race, black people aren't as sound,
Financially, as some others.
To learn empowerment over generations,
We should watch our multi-ethnic brothers.

The first lesson of the dollar,
That should be observed by you and by me.
Is how many times a single dollar changes hands,
Before leaving the Jewish community.

There is a shortage of our own supply;
Although the demand will not stop coming,
And when we see a "black owned" sign, out front,
Most of us will get to running.

Buckle Up

Although not the intention, this may get a round of applause;
I am telling you, flat out, nobody wants to see your nasty draws!
I can't dictate the standard, or determine what you should feel;
I just know you must, first, respect yourself, if anyone else ever will.

We're together in the struggle; I'm saying this because I love you;
With odds already against you, give no reasons for them to judge you.
Believe this like you know this; there is some truth behind it;
How serious should people take you, if pants begin where ass ends?

HTYC

I would be remiss if not mentioning, a key to me coming to be,
Was the time I spent at Essie Lee Floyd Day Care, with HTYC.
Many Saturday mornings, that could've been spend with other stuff,
Were spent learning lessons, of the Hattie Turner Youth Club.

Ms. Mitchell was the truth with the, purpose of youth pursuing unity;
How fitting—we were headquartered, at landmark in the community.
It was standing at the ready, unconsciously, being instilled in me;
To be "Always working especially serving others, minimizing me."

Didn't seem cool to clean Cherry Drive; not everybody was doing it;
But without us knowing it, it taught pride in one's community.
There were the hands of the younger ones, me, Meatball, and Jamal;
The people heard Erin's articulate voice; her face was what they saw.

Interrupt the Negro National Anthem, I won't say it was blasphemy;
What I will say is that, Ms. Mitchell just was not having it.
Lessons seemed inconvenient, but have proved to serve us well;
Teaching us to find a cause, that is greater than ourselves.

I won't belabor the point, but I will say that I'm,
Blessed to be able to say, HTYC taught me to "Lift as I climb!"

Headlights in the Rearview

There's something I've been doing, as long as I've been driving;
You call it watching too many movies; I call it means for surviving.
Opinions on it may differ, with details I will provide;
I will explain it to you, and leave it for you to decide.

Anytime I'm headed to my home, but especially at night,
I check my rearview mirror to see, if I see consistent headlights.
In traffic, cars come and go; many think it's nothing to be thought of;
Maybe it sounds silly, but I make sure I'm not being followed.

If I turn, and they turn, staying behind my car too long,
And I don't recognize them as a neighbor, trust I'm not going home.
I'll shoot down a side street—bust a quick left or a sudden right;
Slow down and speed through yellow, so they get stuck at the light.

Maneuvering through the jumble, I use my wits to best them;
Somebody might get the best of me; I'll be damned if I help them.
So take my advice; always make sure to make a way,
To protect you and your family; don't lead danger to your safe place.

Gambling for Dummies

I wasn't a champion checker player, but I was far from least of,
So I thought nothing of it, when my uncle said the loser buys pizza.
Examining the situation, my eyes got big with thoughts of profit;
I knew my uncle to always carry, plenty of money in his pockets.

For his green, I just knew we were about to have a memorial;
Little did I know, his plan was to give me a tutorial.
Against my mother's objections, and what she had to say,
I sat down at the table, and he said simply, "Shelby, let him play."

He made real light work of me; I can't attribute it to luck;
He showed I thought I knew so much, but hadn't lived long enough.
Usually, a joker, he definitely was not in this instance;
No shucking, jiving, clowning or smiling—he was strictly business.

He seemed to be so confident; I thought him to be bluffing;
I was one pizza in the hole, and he said, "Play double or nothing."
Playing like the "Ice Man," his demeanor was twenty below;
If I sat down with thirty dollars, now, I must've been down to zero.

Looking at his smirk, I asked if he thought it was funny;
He said, "Never gamble with someone if he has the most money."
Learn from what my uncle taught, if you want and so choose;
If you stand a lot to gain, you most likely stand too much to lose.

Slow and Steady

I visited with my granddad; over checkers, we passed lots of time;
Each time we sat to fellowship, I chose to pick his mind.
It seemed he knew much about much—sharp as a tack, I ain't lying;
I could've easily grown discouraged; he beat me time after time.

I asked him how he kept beating me; I took as much as I could stand;
He said, "Hunter I can peep through muddy water and see dry land."
On another day, he said something that would always last:
"You can have what you want out of life; just don't move too fast."

It was like a light bulb went off, prompting me into immediate action;
I slowed down to better think—giving little notice to distractions.
Eight years ago, he died, so it's been that long since I was near him;
From that day to this one, it has resounded; I can still hear him.

I began to contend with him; over time, I even began to beat him;
What else could I do, if I beat a man that I regarded as a genius?
I realized because of his lesson—a great mind, I can be that;
Thinking before I move makes for best actions and less need to react.

On Tithing

In regard to the tithe, it's best that I not deal in lies,
Caught a peak behind the curtain—couldn't believe my eyes.
Not sure if dreams of a mega church, is what caused the actions,
But needless to say, it fueled my immense dissatisfaction.

I'm not naïve enough to think, that any church will be perfect;
It's now a common trend, so not specific to any house of worship.
The pastor and his family are dressed and kept, from head to toe;
But building fund, after many years, has not helped the church grow.

Always an appeal to give—there was never a lack of asking;
Simple amenities like bathrooms and repairs, were always lacking.
It's hard for me to see wrong happening, and remain indifferent;
It was all that I could do, to keep from becoming indignant.

With a want to do what was right, and a limited knowledge,
I vowed not to give to thieves in the temple—instead worthy causes.
Up and coming ministries—campaigns to feed homeless and hungry,
Were the ways in which I began, to tithe when it came to money.

After greater understanding through bible study, I unhanded it;
When I give to God, it's up to those appointed to do as commanded.
Disobedience is not a good defense, if they aren't doing right with it;
I give and leave up to God, how He decides to fix it.

Rival to Iniquity

There'll be the handful that truly love you—
Others that long to dismember you.
But it is not how the people bury you but,
Instead, the way that they remember you.

Some people claim that they give back;
Their claims are far from true.
Me breaking bread is not breaking news,
Because it is what I am known to do.

You can check my resume' if, by chance, you don't believe me;
My benevolence is evident, by the way people receive me.
No stickup man sticking it to the man, I am not a thug, in the club,
Just misunderstood man wanting to understand—a boy needing a hug.

I set out for a new journey,
Hop-scotched the burning sands.
Turned a spark into a flame,
Forced mountains to move with faith and the strain of hands.

I decided to wrestle with mastodons, to better prepare for tests,
Took the emptiest of vessels, and urged them to be the best.
Transformed the unjust into fair, became a rival to iniquity,
Revolutionized the norm, brought acclaim to the world's simplicity.

Sidestepped the seat of honor, and refused to don a throne,
Instead, stayed among common folks, so ego would leave me alone.

Counted Blessings

I looked over the distance,
And noticed it was raining.
Realizing it was to nurture the Earth,
And there was no need in complaining.

Bathing is a cleansing;
Why should Mother Earth not get hers?
A chance to rinse her crevices,
And blossom all of her herbs.

As I looked over the scenery,
I made a mental note to self.
That, though, I might not have a dime,
I've amassed a mass of wealth.

Simple blessings like breath to breathe,
And my prized two eyes to see.
A nose to smell the growing grass,
Sense of touch to feel raindrops on me.

Out of Debt

One night, I laid awake in bed, just staring at the ceiling;
There was nothing hurting me, I just had an eerie feeling.
My stomach felt so settled, I had no aches or pains;
But something wouldn't let me sleep, so I laid there just the same.

As I tried to figure what was wrong, I had an epiphany,
That tomorrow would never come, if I carried yesterday with me.
In order to get most of every minute, maximize daily living,
I'd have to give up grief and grudge, and become more forgiving.

But not just forgiving debtors,
Would make my current feeling be ended.
I needed to apologize for my own debts,
To anyone I may have offended.

There is no way to count up pains;
You may not even know you've hurt someone.
So say you're sorry while you can,
For any wrong you may have done.

Maybe you started a rumor,
All out of spite and hate.
Or perhaps, you broke her heart,
Even though you never dated.

Nothing is promised, in life, but death;
Make it right while you're alive together.
So one of you won't leave before the other,
And you live with regret, forever.

Through the Blur

His plum-colored lips are numb, while his drowsy eyes are red;
Nowhere near a bed, an approaching nap bobs his dreaded head.
Images bleed onto one another; colors blur the scene,
Like static to a radio signal, or broken pixels on a tv screen.

His legs are moving like rubber; feet won't hold fast as they once did,
From what seemed to be a simple taste, has become swig after swig.
Instead of just going to sleep, he does best to make a way,
To thank God for keeping him safe, as he drops to his knees to pray.

Newfound Friend

A young man went and set his stride,
Ever ready to engage in battle, but keeping cool, inside.
He moved so smooth, and without hesitation,
Quick to cold shoulder distraction, and avoid aggravation.

So one night while proguing, all alone in the woods,
He came across some people, that he could do some good.
He saw, as he approached, that they all stood so still;
It was nothing that they possessed—even abandoned by will.

Seemingly trembling, as if approached by a shark,
It became clear the problem was they stood alone in the dark.
They stopped their journey, at dark, and they gave way to doubt;
So the young man intervened, lending a hand to help them out.

Though the young man's figure, had come to them as such a surprise,
Volunteering to lead them, he would, too, be there eyes.
They joined each other's hands, and it was forward that they thrust,
Nothing but servitude to connect them, and a salt grain of trust.

With the young man at the head, came the exit of the group,
And then came showers of thanks, and heartfelt gratitude.
"Young fellow," said an elder, "we could've met with grave danger;
So what made you so noble, willing to help out us strangers?"

"You could have easily left us, afraid and alone in the woods;
Or you could have been a young deviant, out for harm or no good."
So, good fellow, what I am asking, or what I mean to say:
What made you take the time, to be a light and help guide our way?"

"You see, newfound friend, I don't have any funding for college;
So, it's out in this world, that I've set out searching for knowledge.
I've been here for many nights, and have learned a lot, at long last;
I just took what little I know, to try to help light your path."

"And I have found that the key to life,
Can be found within the giving.
For if you have not found what it is you would die for,
What is the point in you living?"

Weeping May Endure a Night

The Labor of a Neighbor

Do me a favor after you read this,
Though it may not be something that you wanna do.
Stand in the nearest mirror,
And take a mental snapshot of what's in front of you.

Be real with the reflection,
As honest as possible when you take it.
Otherwise, you may do something rash,
Possibly displacing the hatred.

Maybe you're envious of someone,
Who accomplished a goal that you've been pursuing.
And you've begun to criticize their success,
Without knowing what they've been doing.

So what if her boyfriend is a prince,
And yours is still a frog.
Or if her hard work has her ready for the beach,
And you feel you could still use a jog.

They may be running to catch their dreams,
While you're only chasing it in your mind.
While they lose sleep helping it come to be,
You just sit around passing the time.

Perhaps, they pray with fervor,
And wait for God to guide their every move.
While you just give a Christmas wish list,
And expect your blessings to find you.

Now, your own insecurities drive your hate—
Keep you mad whenever you're not sad.
And the only culprit is you for wanting,
Instead of living and bettering the life you have.

I've seen it happen, so this is a promise;
I say it without second guessing or doubt.
If you find that you are this person,
This hate will consume you from the inside out.

Hate only begets hate; from it, there will come nothing else,
There's no way to love a neighbor if, inwardly, you despise yourself.

Buzzard Luck

Repo man came to get my car;
Bill collectors won't leave me alone.
Supervisor called me into his office;
Gave me a pink slip, then, he sent me home.

I'm holding on to my job by a thread;
Affirmative action's the only thing that's helping.
I promise; it seems I've been cursed with these curses;
I'm standing in need of a blessing.

My woman just left me the other day;
She says Jody's everything that I'm not.
When she visits him, she isn't scared to get sick,
Because his hot water always runs hot.

Jody took my woman, and she is not looking back;
I left the Joneses alone; now, arthritis wants me down in my back.
I am worked like a borrowed mule; I pace the floor all the night.
I wear cardboard in my shoe bottoms; inconsistency is in my sight.

My glasses got stepped on and, now, they're broke;
That made it extra hard to read my Bible.
Mentioned someone's name in a note I wrote,
Now, they want to sue me for libel.

I saved up to buy me a bicycle;
Minutes later, I got two new flat tires.
Robbers broke in on me and took my things;
What they left behind was burned up in a fire.

Every night, I pray my prayers;
Every day, I sing the blues.
Seems like I have everything to gain,
But I have nothing to lose.

Two Weeks' Notice

How will I impact the world;
How can I ever begin being successful?
When they won't acknowledge my hustle,
And don't appreciate my effort.

Acknowledgment of effort,
Or encouragement of my endeavors.
Could have possibly built a bond,
And kept our ties from being severed.

They should have taken more time, to try and recognize the cost;
So, now, the corporate family will have to mourn the loss.
I'm smiling as I say this, but it is anything but a joke;
I don't mind working for a living, just not for other folks.

I may just be suspicious, but I'm afraid this gig wouldn't last long;
So that's enough motivation, for me to venture out and move on.
It could be a solid premonition, or just a sneaking suspicion;
But whatever it is, it has helped me to come to this decision.

Hunter Johnson Presents…

Success is a journey, and that is a fact;
So, I'm packing my bags, and I refuse to look back.
I've given too long, for them to try and embrace me,
Now, I've given two weeks, for them to try and replace me.

Eff the Rat Race

Trouble is encroaching, and recession is around;
And I am inches away, from almost melting down.
All day long, I'm trapped in a locked maze;
And like it is cheese, it's the paper that I chase.

To anyone who says it's lovely at the top,
My place and his stead, we can swap them.
It may be cold and thin at the top,
But it's hot and crowded down at the bottom.

One thing I must mention,
Because there is one thing I hate.
Because I don't like the scraps that I'm thrown,
I'm chastised and called an ingrate.

It'll be hard for you to understand my trouble;
We aren't in the same class.
I'm one of the ones called by my first name,
And you're referred to by your last.

For you, this is a stipend to live a little,
Until your illustrious career comes alive.
For me, it's a way to keep my lights on—
My very means to survive.

So save yourself the sad eyes,
And please replace the fat face.
Hold in the vain empathy;
I will say eff the rat race.

I am at the depths, it seems;
So how could things get worse?
This cruel condition and unchanging scene,
To me, has run its course.

My restful nights, are outweighed by my restless days;
And, like an inmate, I dream of the time when I can escape.
Though there is no "I" in "TEAM," trust that there is a "me;"
And "Me" is the only man to ensure, that my wife and kids can eat.

I am stuck in the norm,
Wondering how I will pay my bills.
Keep the water and lights turned on,
Provide my kids with school clothes and meals.

A dollar for the drink machine.
A sandwich in my lunch bag.
Is not enough to motivate,
Or keep me from feeling bad.

I will not be fooled;
I'm convinced this is not my curtain call.
I don't wanna just be a water cooler prophet,
Or a noonday know-it-all.

And I am finding,
That no place seems safe.
So I'm saving for a rainy day,
'Til I can say eff the rat race.

Sacks-o-Phone

His number one concern is where he goes to get his pack;
Hitting the interstate, he takes a ride and brings it back.
Just a normal day, it's been normal since it has begun,
The rims on his foreign car, twinkle as they meet the sun.

Riding high, blowing dro, his journey is just so care free;
Not in the least bit shook, though it seems he surely should be.
Why, you ask; he does his task, with the protection of the mob;
But he fails to camouflage his work, foreign cars without a job.

Running around doing the same things,
With no thought to be discreet.
Now, the troopers have put their lights on him;
And the pack's tucked under his seat.

Moral of the story, even when he was away from right,
He cared to make no best attempts, to keep it out of sight.

Vice President

No matter what you're experiencing,
There's no need to subject the world to witnessing.
Outer hate and inner resistance to discipline,
Contributing to the dungeon you're living in.

Bad times make for bad dreams;
And recurring nightmares help to make you crazy.
Cloudy piss and clouds of smoke make vision hazy,
Dancing and riding dirty like Patrick Swayze.

Is it too much to ask for you play your part,
Or to, sometime, stay sober?
Maybe that's what tugs at your heart,
And tends to run your bowels over.

Detriment on the table;
Illegal drugs to help supply the squad.
Hot guns in the closet;
And vicious dogs in the yard.

You were granted ability to change your fate;
Fate's a thing you can't outrun.
Continue on the road you're going,
And it's foolish to expect a new outcome.

It seems you long to ride in a hearse;
To disaster, you've become such a flirt.
Devising these vices, there is no surprise,
Your life has taken a turn for the worse.

Chain Gang

Each step that you make, makes the gold glow a little brighter;
And each rock you break down, lets chain's grips grip you tighter.
Did dirty dealings, were underhanded for gains,
Made a deal with the devil, now, you wear heavy chains.

You really weren't willing,
Although, you were quite able.
Instead of steady shining,
You could have helped your neighbor.

You had ample opportunities,
To bring forth good acts of will.
To replace holes in poor kid's shoes,
Or provide poor folks a meal.

None of this gave you excitement—
Couldn't possibly bring smiles to your face.
Nor could it give you what you craved—
Accolades when you walked in a place.

Now, your destination is chain gang, sundown ever since the sun-up.
'Cause the fuzzy feeling of doing good, for you, was not enough.

Rich and Power Fool

Something "better" came along;
Killer deal so you had to grab it.
Thought you caught a wholesale ticket,
With a fully loaded package.

All because you were fickle,
Direct result of what you chose.
You've found yourself in a pickle,
Much like the emperor's new clothes.

This could be a misunderstanding,
And really could have all been avoided.
But a mere inkling of conceit got peeped,
And, subsequently, it got exploited.

Slight of the hand is not to blame,
Nor downright illusions of the eye.
You became so consumed by the band,
You just let the parade pass you by.

All of the bold-faced lies that you told,
The stiff fingers that you pointed.
Have all seemed to turn back on you,
They all have become double-jointed.

Your frustration is apparent,
'Cause humiliation is immense.
The one you thought to be the court fool,
Proved to be the one with the sense.

Vanity was insanity;
Humbleness, you never took the time to extend it.
Not giving a rip of the hearts you hurt,
Not a damn about those you offended.

Can't help but hear the snickers,
With each footstep and stroke.
To the common subjects, you have become,
Nothing more than a joke.

Should've checked ego at the door,
Setting apart make believe from the truth.
Good emperor, I must admit,
Your new clothes do look good on you.

When you look over the whole situation,
You will see that your money's worthless.
There are many things it serves to buy;
But there is substance it cannot purchase.

Invisible Man

Instead of molding destiny,
He wastes his time with crying.
His potential, he'll never know to show,
Because he doesn't invest in trying.

Trembling on a treadmill,
He presently is not and will never be.
One to stand strong like the trunk,
He's shaky like the leaves of the tree.

He is more than fine with scraps,
Doesn't mind always being looked over.
Flimsy—no resolute bones in his body—
He is a resident pushover.

He's so weak, it is funny—
Comic relief just like a clown.
Most men have nuts like Almond Joys;
But he lacks them like a Mounds.

Pink is the color that fits him best;
He is nobody's formidable contender.
When he does decide to stand his ground,
It's usually toward the female gender.

He has no get-up-and-go, at all;
He is a constant lolly gagger.
Regardless of things that his mouth says,
His image presents him as a straggler.

Never crucial in the clutch,
He chooses a crutch when it comes to critics.
He makes you ask what really is it;
It's almost mystic that he's such a misfit.

To say "son-of-a-bitch" would be wrong;
No Mom insults for birthing from inside them.
To Mom, it's a scratched record and song;
Bitch-of-a-son would better describe him.

But he clings to her ever-feeding breast;
Doubtful if, on his own, he'll ever make it.
And if he happens to make his way,
Somebody will come along and take it.

Maybe, one day, he'll rise like the Phoenix,
And make himself indispensable.
But without change, he'll see the same,
And he'll always stay invisible.

Spinning Wheels

So subconsciously against a change,
They will not know it when they get it.
Won't recognize it as familiar,
They know no one that ever did it.

Diligent with ignorance,
In cess, they have a blissful blast.
They'll almost surely repeat their past;
They aim for no more than they have.

Being thankful is one thing;
It keeps a humble balance and level in.
But there's noticeable difference,
'Tween one reaching and one who's settling.

Limited is a boy or girl,
Who looks up and cannot at least see to the top.
Useless is ambition,
That starts and ends when you hit the clock.

Complacent in current company,
No thought to another day's delight.
Advancement will be made kind of hard,
Since expectancy is so slight.

These people must make changes, now,
If they hope to affect the future.
And know that what exists,
Aren't just the things that they are used to.

No Rubbing Lotion

There's no need in pondering, 'cause only Heaven knows,
What we were born or die for, only God can judge our souls.
We rise with the crowing cock and rest when sun sets out West;
Man lives down here in sin, but aims and strives to be the best.

Longing to be more like a hero,
Nothing less than a winner.
Progressing more and more,
Each day I survive, still destined to be a sinner.

And the strife, in this life, I search for escape,
So I can, one day, be leaving.
But I am determined it is here to stay,
Each second that I remain breathing.

Tears come with friends;
Misery loves company; they are never alone.
Problems and troubles come in bulk and in pairs;
And, it seems, they never get gone.

Each nook, crook, cranny, crevice—every faucet is filled with acid;
No need to rub in lotion, engulf, instead, in prophylactics.

My People

My people saw chains, and my people saw hoses;
My people were whipped and punched in their noses.
My people were tried and convicted, regardless of their innocence;
They were exploited and used, rendered helpless without defense.

From a long line of royalty, in the land from which they came,
They were bound down with shackles and stripped of their names.
They were forced to say "Master" and answer questions with "Sir,"
Sometimes given things, not fit for fowls of the Earth.

Sometimes, scared to sing out,
Because their owners made them fear them.
They would begin to moan their hymns,
So the devil could not hear them.

As day moved to night and night moved to day,
They knew that God, would surely make a way.
After the Civil War, what will happen, no one knows,
Lincoln played Moses, and let my people go.

Then, there was The Movement,
Tryin' to let off some steam.
And in came Martin Luther King,
The smart preacher from Atlanta, with his dream.

King was forced to die,
Because of hate and ill relation.
Not before speaking—
Shocking the world and changing the nation.

Now, my people are day's strength and nighttime's valued pearls,
Sitting atop the hill, the kings and queens of the world.

One More Step

I speak about my ancestors,
From days since long gone.
Stripped from their freedom,
As they were snatched from their homes.

A legacy of royalty, is one from which they came,
Slave traders ended reign, when they bound them all to chains.
Through the great wrath of the storm, and the coldness of the rain,
My people stood strong, through the obstacles and pain.

In an unjust world, forced to succumb to their fears,
They faithfully prayed for salvation, while slaving in the fields.
Some were lynched and mobbed, or beaten to their graves,
Choosing, sometimes, death, rather than to be a slave.

As the new century rolled in, and the old one sizzled out,
Prejudice rode backseat, in the North, but thrived deep in the South.
Then came a young leader—a strong man with a dream;
Equality was coming, just not fast as it seemed.

He said that days to come,
Shouldn't resemble those of the past,
That some day brotherhood would lead,
Our people to have freedom, at last.

Then, one fateful April day, through prejudice, hatred, and spite,
A single gunshot to the head, ended that young man's life.
Riots made way to streets; peaceful protesters continued to pray,
Joining hands and singing, "We shall overcome, some day."

Now that the waters are calmed, and prejudice is at ease,
We are one step closer, to achieving the King's dream.

Felt the Effects

Though we have overcome, some of the troubles of the past,
We may not truly say, that we are really free at last.
Now that black men and white men can fellowship with each other,
Some of us black folks still seem to hate one another.

Do not be ashamed; our life story could uncover,
That we have all been guilty, at one time or another.
Those of us that tend to skin and grin, then, gossip from a distance,
Cuss the preacher for taking collection, and claim to be biggest Christians.

Jealousy is evident; the ignorance is apparent, but the motives are unclear;
Taking a high and mighty approach and thinking others are way down here.
We should not have trumped up words and arrogant stares,
Enjoy the blessed life, now, lest we forget our toils and snares.

We have all felt the effect, the whirl of the wrath,
And we've all trod down, the same unyielding path.
Even a naïve man, raised by wolves in a cave,
Would know, fair skinned or dark, most black Americans were slaves.

This should not be an issue—a subject shunned from the discussion;
If we don't open our eyes and minds, we will reap the repercussions.
Black on black crime is at an all-time high, too many armed and robbed,
Supposedly dying to live, seemingly, living to die, doing the Klansman's job.

There is no need to worry, no reason to cause a panic,
But if there is no change, we will sink like the Titanic.
We are a hustling tribe of professionals and scribes;
We've waited all this time, and our day has arrived.

Just like the sun shines yellow, and we all bleed red,
Sure as we are living, now, some day, we'll all be dead.
Remembering the good with the bad—the books with the tools,
We traveled this far, by faith; now's no time to be fools.

No Pot to Piss

I know the trap well; I was born in it and bred in it,
Not where the craps swell, with the bodies found dead in it.
No, it's the one everybody has to face, each and every day,
And the same one, that, sometimes, seems like it lacks a way.

I'm the one on the corner with a fat little sack,
Saying, "Eat with your boy," 'til you feel too fat.
Last thing on my mind, is to give your nose its treat,
Only grass I know, is what to cut, just to make ends meet.

The clenched fist in the air screaming, "Power to the people,"
I'm the bowed down head giving glory to the steeple.
Fifty brownies in the sleeve, when the change gets wrapped,
Salty sweat in the bread winner's baseball cap.

The bologna in the fridge, when there's no money for the ham,
I'm viennas and sardines and the canned loaf SPAM.
The choice not to sell dope, saying, "I'd rather be broke,"
Live in the twilight dim, but I am a bright ray of hope.

I too know the strip, and I too know the club,
Not the one making up to girls for daddy's negated love.
Instead, the strip where everybody looks for refund checks,
The club that don't know shit about the "stacks on deck."

Not the "G" in the streets, or sliding down a gold pole,
Instead, the "B" student grinding hard, just to buy cheap clothes.
Aside from glitter and the singles and the tall stack heels,
I'm the McDonald's check that just does pay bills.

I'm abstract, and that's a fact, I'm not what you can touch,
Just in the hearts of struggling folks, you won't see me much.
The silver lining, ever-shining through the gloomy clouds of doubt,
Smiling still, with no pot to piss, or window to throw it out.

Po' Mouth

The doctor and me ain't on speakin' terms;
I ain't seen no dentist in a minute.
No knowledge, at all, of cholesterol;
Sugar intake—I couldn't tell you the limit.

Copay's, to some, a burden; but, myself, I wouldn't mind,
If affording insurance, wasn't such a thorn in my side.
My liver is of concern; I won't lie, sometime, I sip;
It is therapy I can afford; the other kind I just can't wrestle with.

Gym memberships are too high;
My body's aging and will not wait.
So I stretch and exercise,
To try and pull me into shape.

Oh, if I could have back the days,
Of my childhood and I was a boy when.
I had no worries of payin' bills;
What a time of life's enjoyment.

The shadow of debt dwindles my days;
Having not grinds away my nights.
Worries have given me wrinkle lines;
Stress has turned my few black hairs to white.

Classism clouds my compassion;
Fighting envy strips me of energy.
And all I can do is thank the good Lawd,
That He strengthens me with serenity.

Potted Meat and Noodles

Let's hit a home run,
On whatever the present may throw us.
Grab life by the collar,
So we can get what it owes us.

This is a tale of outlet,
And a form of expression facet.
For folks that have lived all their lives,
Not knowing what it feels like to have shit.

The economy is unstable,
But you can just sit back and laugh.
Not worrying about a thing at all,
You know how it feels to not have.

Never will you feel like a loser;
No one can make you not a winner.
You remember potted meat for lunch;
Ramen noodles often served as your dinner.

In these hard and troubled times,
You had better count your blessings.
If you don't, you'll find, at times,
It gets downright bad and depressing.

Drudging in the badness,
Wading in a proverbial sewer.
Dwelling in the madness,
Sloshing through the bull manure.

Seed and Feed

There was nothing clouding my vision,
Just twinkling stars I could see.
Never on Earth did I imagine,
The travesty, soon, to come to me.

I had seen it happen to sisters;
And alike, it happened to brothers.
And though, it never beset me,
I empathized when it happened to others.

Now, my time had come;
And there was no way for me to avoid it.
At the time, I didn't want to;
In fact, I really implored it.

There was this young pearl—not just booty, true beauty—
A real ebony flower.
A true, true treasure—a diamond, no rough,
So I pursued many days and many hours.

To my surprise, when she realized,
I was what she wanted, or more, she needed.
She came to me, with humility,
Not a little stuck up or a bit conceited.

One thing led to another; things got heated;
Moans and groans filled the room.
In about a minute, I'd be on and in it,
And inside her glistening womb.

Becoming greater and greater with each good stroke,
This is realer than any truth I've spoke.
It came as sudden as a lump in my throat;
And in a quick "pop," the rubber, it broke.

I kept doing what I was doing,
In bliss, no grieving;
Not knowing her motherly duct,
Was filled with my seamen.

When I looked down and noticed,
I had mixed emotions, some drama.
My only regret at the time was,
Somehow, I would have to tell my mama.

The end of the world, no,
But sometimes, the dough gets low.
Nine to five or knockin' hustles,
I have to feed my seed either way that it goes.

Although the pain that my loins deployed,
Today, are untimely and incredible.
There's still room for gain and joy,
But, now, manhood has become inevitable.

Coping

Like class in session, life will teach you a lesson,
The plan, not your discretion, necessarily the essence.
Hard knocks and bumps, pass drops and humps,
Pain is what we're born in, but what is YOUR response?

Problems ain't systematic, like splinters in an attic,
Coming by the plenty, like snow on shows, that just catch static.
I moved up laughing and trumped up joking,
Stepped up drinking, and picked up smoking.

Even with the stress, I never did start doping,
But sometimes smoked squares, 'til my chest started choking.
Words kept to myself, most times unspoken,
Just did what I had to, to proceed in coping.

Imagine the strife, in life, you face,
Issues of emotion, money, place, and race.
Punching the clock, daily, trying to make a living,
Greedy friends, constantly, reaching with no giving.

The pushing and the pulling, the tugs and the snatches,
The struggle that you face, like making fire with no matches.
Got away from the lows, by setting the bar a little higher,
Flipped off despair, and called the devil a liar.

Used a new ruler, so I could measure success,
Moved a little cooler, so I could be my best.
Dreamed a little harder, for the things I've been hoping,
And all of this was done, as a method of coping.

Here, I Stand

I stand willing to take my convictions,
All of my sentencing and reproofs.
Armed with no compelling evidence,
And equipped with nothing but truth.

My nights seem slim, while my days grow longer,
My down time is less and less.
Fight, in my heart, is fueled by my hunger,
To strive for and take nothing less than best.

The struggles that I face from day to day,
They keep me weary, out on my feet.
Like a muzzle strapped on a bulldog's face,
I stay silent with anguish—discreet.

Nobody knows the trouble I see;
Nobody can fathom my sorrow.
Nobody knows that pain doubles at me;
That's why I invest in tomorrow.

Inherited this life, a silent prayer to comfort,
On my imaginings, I relied to thrill me.
Just imagine my strife, speech articulate, but jumbled,
I'll be somebody, some day, if it kills me.

North and Southbound Friendship

Seems like the ceiling's coming down, and the walls are closing in,
As I realize and analyze, the true plights of all my friends.
Some love whole-heartedly, and some never seem to begin;
Some seem to fade away, when good times and fast women end.

Secrets kept close to the heart, breathed not a word of it, discreet,
And if I ever had a piece of bread, I broke it, so we all could eat.
I got dragged into the beefs, all for the sake of loyalty;
Imagine the cease of peace I've seen, clutched my pistol just to go to sleep.

Don't take this as petition, or a plea or cry trying to implore you;
Because I'll still stand if I see tomorrow, as the man I was before you.
This question doesn't need an answer; it is rhetorical in a way;
Are you true to those true to you, what kind of friend are you, today?

Contradicting Character

If you could, you would claim transparency,
Anytime someone chose to ask.
Remember the thing about glass houses is,
It's easy to smudge the glass.

The image that you display to all, seems so sincere;
You make it seem true.
But what happens when your house doors close;
And no one's there to see what you do?

I've given careful thought to this,
And hope, from it, you'll benefit.
Since we've all sinned and come short,
The worst thing we can be is a hypocrite.

We all have imperfections;
I'll be the first fellow to admit it.
Every day we live is an evolution;
So let's not condemn others as if we never did it.

Whatever you choose to do is your business,
Because you are your own person.
Just don't be the one that can't wait to blame,
For the same thing that you are, privately, indulging.

Anything you are dealing with,
God will fix on His time by His design.
But we only compound our sins,
When we couple them with hypocrisy and lying.

I would be a fool to think about scolding you,
Because I want to be recognized and highly viewed.
If, when I get behind closed doors,
I'm doing more of that thing than you do.

So, before you think that it's fine and dandy to shun, in public,
What you do, privately, at home.
Remember, God not only hears what you say to people,
But sees what you do, alone.

Gertrude the Gossip

She feels compelled to tell it, now;
She just can't wait 'til later.
And she brings new meaning,
To the term "nosy neighbor."

She knows who's sleeping with the teacher,
And waking up with the preacher.
If the Feds ever relocated a snitch,
Gertrude the Gossip could probably reach her.

In any event, she always knows the why and the when;
Time is spent digging for dirt, cackling on the phone like a hen.
Talking about Joanna strips, and that's how she pays her bills,
And that Danny's son and baby girl, really aren't his.

All Gertrude wants is the juice;
She has no use for facts.
Just like that dog brought a bone,
That dog will take one back.

So before you go telling Gertrude your business,
Even though you think she is your girl.
Remember she loves gossip more than she loves you,
And is known to keep mess stirred.

Outside

It is looking bad;
I got sad when I looked out over the community.
I see it as it is, now,
And wrap my mind around how it used to be.

The neighborhood bum standing on the corner,
Trying to make a dollar to buy a drink.
Old as he is, with all his petty charges,
It seems he should've learned, you'd think.

Yonder, over there, look;
It is the neighborhood drug dealer.
He's riding in his fancy car;
And he's steadily getting richer.

What you don't see,
Is his best customer is not getting any bigger.
He's getting money, girls, and fame—
Killing his people and taking away male figures.

Fitness for Life

The tiger's in the jungle, and the panther's on the prowl;
Feasting time is signified, by the hooting of the owl.
The slithering snakes are steadfast, in hunting for a meal;
The innocent prey are dead last; the predators are on their heels.

And the silence of the surroundings, is like a wave before it's tidal;
The actions that are yet to come, are in the interest of survival.
The wind and the rain and the clap of the thunder,
Do not compare, by far, to a night in the jungle.

Many give chase, while many others, end up dead;
By stealth and strategy, inevitable bloodshed.
With the fire and the howls and, yet, the silence of revival,
The fit of the flock will, in turn, collect the best survival.

The corner is a hustle, dominated by the dime;
Filled to the realm of vast rewards, but dictated by the times.
The dope dealer is, no doubt, on a mission to get it;
To feed a family or trick out a car, his profession, to him, is fitted.

The origin of crack, the poor man's drug,
Represented a gangster's reprisal.
Penitentiary chances, he's willing to take,
For an attempt at his survival.

His efforts to eat, no room for defeat—
A constant race with the clock.
While he's sacking the weed and bagging the blow,
Constantly whipping the rock.

It's seldom he eats, always going,
Junkies always seem to find him.
Boppers stay bopping, counting his pockets,
And the law, a step behind him.

A gun-slinging cowboy, if it arises—
An OK Corral shooting Fivel.
The decisions he's made, in his mind,
For the best, most hope for his mere survival.

The sun's set westward, and fluorescent lights,
Make it seem, like forever, it is day.
Band's in stands--cocked, locked, and ready;
The fight song is the song that they play.

The objective, at hand, with the game plan, they have come to grips,
Some are in it to win it, some for big hits, but others for scholarships.
Unleashed like greyhounds on a track, or a pack of hungry tigers,
When the ball is snapped, everything else, for survival.

All hell breaks loose, when straps secure the "hut,"
Whether blind-sided crack or corner back pedaling up.
To be afraid or timid, for here, there is no time,
When ball is in play, after stretching, it is show time.

Inappropriate to go slow mo,' or even worse, stand there, idle,
Maybe somewhere else, but the name of this game is survival.

Necessary Roughness

The whistling of the winds, they entertain the night;
And the car horns sound like trumpets, blowing against the lights.
Everybody is choosing his poison, leaning in his or her own way,
The weak begging for mercy; the predators, stalking their prey.

The vices of the twilight, saturate the cold city streets;
The bosses live the high life; while the cops, they walk the beat.
I see a victim in my sights; I know that she is a goner;
By the look on her face I can tell, as I watch her from the corner.

She is lost deep in her innocence; so curious, yet, she's so timid;
Full-grown woman, full of grace and beauty, to the game, an infant.
She has noticed me watching her; I see her through smoke and fog;
Catching her eye, without a word, I have, yet, to step from my hog.

She tries to avoid the temptation,
As she tries to pass me by, quickly.
I have to cop her before someone else;
I open my door and begin to go to her, swiftly.

When she looks at me, it's clear that she does not see,
Any of that bull squares believe, or what they show on TV.
Instead of great big hats and long nails, or platform shoes,
Diamonds on cups, pimp sticks and the fried up hairdos.

She sees a stand-up guy with confidence in abundance;
Who doesn't like to work, but needs to pay his rent.
So he takes what he has, and he uses what he knows;
Respect is what he commands; charisma is what he shows.

He makes sense when he speaks, and he talks kind of quick;
He's a silky smooth 'Nova, sultry son of a bitch.
Knows what is right, but continues to do wrong,
Perhaps, wants to change, but has been at it for so long.

A thinking man of logistics, he is a stickler for reason;
A dog, to the heart, his flower's never out of season.
When all's said and done, he'll smile; so believe when he says it,
"Pimpin' definitely ain't easy, but it's very necessary."

Closed for Business

A cool winter night, and he needs to find a hit;
He's messed around, and got strung out on that shit.
Saw his neighbor, earlier; neighbor advised he get a job;
His habit will not wait for that; it's better that he steal and rob.

In beginning planning phases,
He has plans to cross the tracks.
But if he carries out his plans,
It'll be hard to travel back.

Getaway could prove to be a snag,
And foil his plans of armed robbery.
If he does his crime at his store of choice,
Tough patrons will not let him leave.

What can he do besides reconsider;
Go somewhere and think his plan through.
He's got all he needs, just needs a target,
Somewhere he can point and shoot.

The longer he considers his destination,
The more the nighttime just keeps on falling.
As the night grows long and the time rolls on,
The more his habit just keeps on calling.

It's tapping and tugging; he can't sit still—
Needs his medicine and can't hardly stand it.
The first store he comes to, he's going in;
For the money, he's going to demand it.

He tells his homeboy to come walk with him;
In a hurry, there's no time to waste.
Gotta make it up to the corner store,
The lady that runs it usually stays open late.

He runs the idea by his bosom buddy,
As they are approaching the store's front.
His friend turns to walk away from there;
That's not the kind of trouble he wants.

Davis, we will call him,
Watched his friend walk out of sight.
Nerve mixed with unbearable yearning,
Lets him know that the time is right.

No mask on his face, just pistol in hand;
He began to scream, all his slurred-speech demands.
Her back was to his barrel; cooperating, her hands were up;
But she wasn't giving up the money, to young Davis, fast enough.

He shot her several times; like a phantom never there, he was gone,
With a few new dollars in pocket, that he could go get high on.
People were running and screaming, getting out fast, no wasting time,
When an unfamiliar sight began to register in their minds.

And the most unlikely person,
Who wouldn't leave her side 'til relieved by cops.
Was who everyone would call a bum,
The alcoholic from down the block.

Davis turned the town upside down, if not but for a brief instant;
Apprehended a short time after, he left the store closed for business.

Shattered

Manifested for the hardwood,
Predestined to the limelight.
Joe was a sure win for good;
He just had to get his mind right.

Recruited since an early age,
Each time he jumped, he took flight.
He made any court his center stage;
But he loved to hang and liked to fight.

The guys on the team with Joe,
Seemed just too lame and far too slow.
Didn't know how to make that green,
They didn't know how to "mack the hoes."

So Joe did his thing, trying to get paid;
He found himself intertwined.
Trying to get himself some bling bling,
He started out with nicks and dimes.

His performance, as always, was superb and as expected;
He had his game, so his profession, no one ever suspected.
The dimes suddenly seemed confined; he moved on to bigger things,
For his blow, they stood in line; he even moved to Promethazine.

The clout, he had it, and it became nothing for him to get a woman;
The scouts visited every game, so the cheese was surely coming.
One night, he was walking slow, freshly back from serving blow;
His fat cash flow, made his pants sag kind of low.

Joe heard the cocking hammer—felt the barrel beside his head;
It was a guy in a black hoodie; one false move and Joe was dead.
He told Joe to lay it down, if he wanted to live,
And anything of any value, is what Joe was to give.

Joe had had an entire career, and never choked in the clutch;
But the lifestyle he had chosen, for him, now, became too much.
If it had been a first step, Joe could have hit it, quick;
Instead, this time, he was too slow; Joe hesitated a bit.

Within just an instant, the gunman had shattered Joe's dreams,
Killing the most potential, the neighborhood had ever seen.
Maybe, one day, Joe's folks would have a chance for another,
But the body of the present, lay bloody and dying in the gutter.

Fix Me

The man stands and looks for ways through closed doors;
Until this point, a jungle, his life has been.
New life away from smoking weed and paying whores,
In and out of the system, since the age of thirteen.

He wants to change his life and make it right;
"I guess, now, you'll scream that you're saved."
His friends rag him 'cause he won't slang and fight,
Wants to do better than his younger days.

The man will not deny or tell a lie,
As his friends' jokes start getting worse.
Declares he's not a saint but will still try,
Needs more than beer to quench his thirst.

He wanted a drink from the refrigerator,
Turning to catch a falling fork.
Intending to return just a moment later,
He heard gunshots riddle his friends, on the porch.

Running out to make sure his friends were alive,
He thinks "it is my attempted change that let the reaper miss me."
Saddened and surprised—not even the largest survived,
He fell to his knees and said, "Lord, Jesus, fix me."

Joy Cometh in the Morning

Life's Best Lessons

I'm learning life's best lessons, from the soldiers of days of old,
And how to deal with the thing, that grips my gut and rips my soul.
I've learned best way to get back, is not extending the vengeance,
Instead, seeking healing I am lent, when giving my repentance.

Even in my dimmest hour, down and out getting slaughtered,
I knew enough to recall two words, and call on "Our Father."
I'm all about His precious love; it covers me, and I ever feel it;
He is savior of my troubled soul, and uplifter of my spirit.

Engineer in the Booth

There aren't variables to weigh, no sides of which to wrestle;
There is no secret to my success; I'll gladly tell you I'm just a vessel.
God is the engineer inside the booth—the conductor of this train,
He just allows me to be a part; I'm here to glorify His name.

Ain't no question or suggesting;
I would not be anything without Him.
It is such a refreshing blessing, that what He does through me,
No one can do anything about it.

Oh, the comfort in knowing,
There is nowhere he cannot lift me.
And should I start to "smell myself,"
He can humble me and whip me.

Destiny's Calling

After ten years of faithful service,
You had no way to know.
That when it came time for layoffs,
You would be the first to go.

So you occupied your abundant time,
With the hobby you love to do.
And from it, came a business where you're your own boss—
See how God looked out for you?

You had a long-term relationship;
You did all you could to patch and mend it.
So, naturally, it almost broke you into pieces,
When it, finally, ended.

His commitment never matched yours;
Family and friends noticed as much.
But if it wasn't for the bad boy of your past,
Would your current good man still mean as much?

Your college career was on a downward spiral;
Your trophy girl always wanted your eyes on her.
But one day, your eye got caught,
On the shy nerdy girl sitting over in the corner.

With yourself, you were at odds,
Wondering did you choose to settle.
But your new girl never brings you down;
She's elevated you to her level.

I won't be cliché and say "God's always on time,"
Because it is so often said.
I'll just point out Jesus didn't go visit Lazarus,
Until after Lazarus was dead.

See, we can't case God;
Just have faith He is interested in our fate.
You may not see Him at His desk, always,
But He always works and is never late.

What we think is ideal,
And would like to see in our hands is.
A product of our human nature,
And our limited understanding.

Your destiny is calling;
So don't sweat what you can't control, anymore.
Just move and know it's God working His will—
Preparing what He has in store.

Lessons in Listening

Experts say that, in communication, the piece that is so often missing,
Is that everyone wants to talk, but many people, seldom, volunteer to listen.
You can argue it however you want to but, still, I am convinced;
Speaking without listening, is where the disconnect comes in.

In all areas of life, lacking listening in communication can deceive us,
In relationships and at work—even when we try to have a talk with Jesus.
Humor me for just a second, and, maybe, you will come to see,
The reason that you don't see God's hand, is you fail to hear Him speak.

You ask the Lord to bless you with money, health, gifts, and such,
But won't give Him time to respond, and tell you where to pick them up.
Try this: when you send up requests, like a child's wish list, at Christmas,
Pause in your petition, and just take a few minutes to listen in.

(I Believe…)

Most people will tell you, if you want it that you should claim it;
How about doing your part, instead of feeling all you should do is name it?
Find a quiet place for quiet time; don't let asking be your only action,
It's hard to get your answer, amidst a world of distractions.

Hunter Johnson Presents…

That speaking that you're listening for, probably won't be a booming voice,
Instead, a stirring of spirit in your soul, that influences your choice.
The advice you get from God is sound; His wisdom is infinite and lasting;
If you won't take the time to hear His answers, what is the point of asking?

Through this Barren Land

I'm just a stranger in this land—a pilgrim in this place,
Living and learning forgiving, wanna meet Jesus face-to-face.
Not a hypocrite, at all; this is really me;
I am far from perfect, but He's in the process of fixing me.

I will never be perfect, but can strive to get close,
Still, not as far progressed as some, but more willing than most.
I know to start the revival process, to be about forward progression,
First, we have to stand and take, steps in the right direction.

Try to love my neighbor, like I love my reflection,
Acceptance, never rejection, smiles and hugs when needing affection.
Maybe He will say "well done," when I get to the gate,
If I try to remedy with love, instead of harboring hate.

All the King's Men

As a child, I sang,
"This little light of mine, I'm gonna let it shine."
But understanding just what this means,
Had to come with time.

I started praying for understanding and,
In the Bible, looking around.
So it's begun to come clear, after all these years;
Now, I'll share what I have found.

There are spiritual gifts called talents,
That are given, freely, and embedded within us.
Though not everyone has been called to be a preacher,
All of us are called to minister.

Because it is his calling,
A preacher gives God's word from the pulpit, on Sunday.
But the need for ministry is always there,
And not reserved for only one day.

Maybe, you have an anointed voice,
That is uplifting to hear.
That can make a non-believer know Jesus loves them—
Your voice says it's sincere.

Perhaps your spirit is such a comfort,
That it seems to be unreal.
Able to provide comfort to the terminally ill,
Even while knowing they'll never be healed.

Your hands may be blessed in a way,
That allows you to feed your hungry brethren.
Opening his eyes to know what more lies in store,
If he will eat the bread of Heaven.

The point of all of this,
Is your shining light doesn't have to be preaching or singing.
But that does not mean,
God hasn't equipped all His people to expand His kingdom.

God's Giving

I've done a bit of re-reading,
So I can better understand the design.
And do as close to what was intended,
When Jacob made a covenant to tithe.

I have heard interpretation,
Saying that ten percent is valid.
Many speak of the currency but,
Yet, neglect the time and the talent.

They clench their fists closed shut;
And never, once, do they reckon.
That they are being blessed,
In order that they can be a blessing.

A man with open palms,
Praising while kneeling on the ground.
Should receive what God intended,
Rise to his feet, and pass it all around.

Material things are tangible,
But I've never known to miss expensive trips.
But do know and am touched and shown,
His most divinely inspired gifts.

Give up all belongings—
Even your life, in pursuit of a new one.
I'd rather be a broke man, in worldly possessions,
Than to be a broken human.

Being a good steward of His blessings,
Makes Him trust you with even more.
That you have not room enough to receive,
Or no place to try and store.

Not only will it be an extension of a blessing,
And obedience for Him to smile on.
It will increase your talent through practice,
Like iron sharpening iron.

Soil Seeking Till

You've escaped the clutch of death—
Defied the odds more times than most.
Allowed to be passed over like you've marked, with blood—
The lats of your door post.

Sidestepping missiles of addiction,
You have become better equipped.
Character on stand in trials of fire,
Your heart's tempered from bad relationships.

Financially rebounded after taking long shots,
But you always find sighs of relief.
You've walked through Death's shadowy valley,
But still resist the Prince of Peace.

He has blessed and continuously kept you,
But you refuse to open eyes to see.
That there could be a reason that,
Now, you still remain to be.

Be like a drain seeking rain,
Or the soil seeking till.
Though you are scarred of the world,
Do not be scared of the will.

Maybe you are missing what's being revealed,
As He does His holy will.
But you are here and shouldn't want to leave,
Until your calling has been revealed.

Displays of Faith

Before, I explained that life, to me, is borrowed time;
I may not see three scores and ten, so better say what's on my mind.
Each day you rise, and can see the world through your eyes,
It should be proof to the doubter, that there is a God in the sky.

How ignorant of some, to not believe until they're shown,
Never seen Fort Knox, but you believe it's full of gold.
My hope is for you, to put to work the things you say;
Actions over spoken words are, always, better displays of faith.

Personally, when I feel like there is something, that is tugging at me,
I pray until I am convinced, it is something more than just me.
Determined to be truly faithful, not only in speech but in my deeds,
I will go any and everywhere, that the Holy Spirit leads.

Let You Steer

Lord, please grant me the strength and the serenity,
Wisdom and virility, to be the man that's really me.
And, too, show me what I need to know;
Anoint that seed so it'll help me to grow.

If it seems that I have come to my wick's end,
Let me gather myself, so that I can breathe again.
If trouble comes, please keep me from stress and outward acting,
Just as you protected me from cracking, and the perils of trapping.

I know that you, indeed, have a plan for my life,
And will give it, in turn, like you gave me my wife.
If not, then, I'm sure you'd not brought me here,
So I'll take my hands off of the wheel, and I will let you steer.

DVD Extra

When you bring home a DVD,
You get more than theaters let you.
Sometimes, commentary and director's cuts—
Different things comprising the extras.

As I looked over the scene,
The most interesting thing that I thought of.
Was how much work goes on behind the scenes,
In order to get the finished product.

Most of us only care to see the movie—
Never mind what has to come, first.
Have you thought as is with film producers,
Is the same with the director of the universe?

As we go about our normal lives,
We can see the end coming, never.
What we don't realize is God's behind the scenes,
For us, making it all come together.

Did you think it was coincidence,
You heard about the job opening, while standing in line?
Imagine what all had to happen,
For you all to be in the same place, at the very same time.

Was it by chance or luck,
That day that you found money in the street?
No; God let the wind blow it to you—
He knew you needed help for the ends to meet.

Things didn't happen the way you thought;
But it just was not the time.
There were too many circumstances to be touched,
So that your thing could fall in line.

So be at peace with what you possess,
Until you see the premiere of the plethora.
Because our director's hard at work,
He's **DiV**ine and **D**oing **Extra.**

Short Arms and Small Hands

It's said that no man knows the day;
The hour is known to no one.
So we should remain ready,
Because death cannot be undone.

What's the use in pondering;
There's no need to wonder how.
God took care of olden day pilgrims;
So what would be different, now?

I'm skeptical of giving "sound" advice,
For fear that it may fail you.
So I am truthful,
Since God has given me a testimony to tell you.

Caution should be a passionate habit to master;
Practicing patience bypasses pain.
There would be a lot less wrecks if,
Everyone would stay in their lane.

I am just a man, and my hands are really tied;
So I leave it in God's hands, because His are way bigger than mine.

The Land Promised Us

It is written God's people would outnumber,
The beach's sand grains or stars in the sky.
In regard to that truthful promise,
I assume we're meant to be great—destined to shine.

You can't believe he or she,
Will be least because, currently, they are less.
Maybe with refinement—purifying, in time,
Will let them go from less to best.

It's promised we'll feast on milk and honey;
Land promised our fathers is where we'll stop.
Staying humble, when we get quail from the sky,
And manna from Heaven and water from a rock.

Faithful, we'll follow the cloud, by day,
Pillar of fire, by night.
Finding something we can hold on to,
Getting a grip to hold on tight.

He gave the sweat of my brow, so I'll know what work is,
Refreshing oases of water, when I know what thirst is.
The grace of good health, given as a means to survive,
Warm blood in my veins, so I'd know that I am alive.

Grace so amazing, I would have a reason to bow,
Passionate strength and clear vision, so I can get through the "now."
Emotions and tears, to determine my feelings,
Prayerful meditation, when my soul needs some healing.

More Than Conquerors

Set the Woods on Fire

Giving until I'm spent,
Way past the point of just being tired.
Most ever-present goal,
Was to set the woods on fire.

No, not a forest fire;
I was advised to try and prevent it.
But burning a massive flame,
Like a lightning strike might have hit it.

I knew I would encounter,
Life's trials and venomous hate.
But I straddled my saddle,
Fit for Alexander the Great.

With as much control,
As any good horse trainer could want.
I stood mine on his hind legs,
Just to see him spar the air in the front.

I ran my hand threw my dampened head,
Wiped the sweat from my sun-beaten brow.
My work had begun long before;
But help wouldn't wait 'til later and was needed now.

On my blazing saddle, so quiet,
I seemed like a phantom.
Heading to the forest,
With heart and love for reckless abandon.

My fifteen minutes in the light,
Some would call a chance to shine.
But I call it a medium,
To better help those of my time.

Love was my motivation,
And helped me on my journey without a pause.
Just the idea that I could enlighten,
And to further a worthy cause.

I chose to give it as I received it,
Had to teach it as I learned.
I try to live it as I perceive it,
And it is this that I have earned.

Looked at to help fill,
All of the needs of the game.
So it is plain to see,
It was my deeds that fanned the flames.

Inventory of Myself

I accumulated good rapport, and built a cloud of clout,
But I am devilishly defiant.
I am, quite often, as quiet as a church mouse,
Sometimes, roaring like a mountain lion.

My mood is cool and smooth,
Not just a regular dude.
Unafraid of caring or sharing,
Indulging what no one would dare to do.

(You know me…)

I'm the life in the grass;
I'm the thread of the shirt.
Like the head of the class,
I'm the high in the "purp."

Family in the reunion,
I'm the bond between kin folks.
Considered the labor in the union,
I'm the howl of the wind blow.

Standing tall and ever strong,
Like what a tree trunk should be.
I'm never off and always on,
Always where I said I would be.

Who really feels my pain;
So often, I've tried to hide.
A vice of mine, I can't explain;
It is my foolish pride.

(I'll say…)

I am a phenom of my time,
And a prodigy of knowledge.
A real master of the mind,
A walking advertisement for college.

I am the "go" in the "bingo,"
And the "toot" in the flute.
I am a fellow in "the know,"
Example of fruit respecting root.

Obligation is a must;
I am the portrait of duty.
Non-violent protester, sure,
But they are coming to shoot me.

Deadly as a snake bite,
I try to cage my rage.
One thing that it might,
Just be me coming of age.

(That's that…)

A ventriloquist with emotion—
Talented tenth, like a tithe.
I am poetry in motion—
A smooth Cadillac ride.

I'm a six-shooting gunner;
My arm declares I am "The Truth."
Some prefer to say "Hunter J,"
While some just call me "that Que."

Non-fictitious, but vicious,
It's hard not to respect me.
I taste success; it's delicious;
It's my Father that protects me.

Put the "haves" and "have nots,"
All together in one body.
Show the hope and shun the dope,
Like Jesse says, "I am somebody."

Knee-Deep

A young country boy, he hustled and grinded,
Swore to make a way, if he could not find it.
So he coupled his talents, with his will and his drive,
Praising God, daily, for the means to survive.

It was the small pleasures, in his life and his brain,
That kept that young boy, from going insane.
The laugh made it light, pain much less to withstand,
While that young country boy, moved from boy to a man.

People ridiculed; they pointed and picked,
But he kept his head straight, through thin and the thick.
What's last will be first, and the Bible says that;
Not sure of what verse, but this proves that it's fact.

Often the northbound end of a southbound joke,
Now, the boy's living life, while the jokers are still broke.
Making hard knocks recreation, playing his cards like a sport,
With only a prayer to pray, and his folks there for support.

Subject of the sentence, object of discussion,
Contagious like the common cold, an obsession like compulsion.
Yet and still, with an iron will, ever-standing like the Vulcan,
So shocking and amazing, sent the world into convulsions.

Intruded on inner sanctums, to learn the tricks of the trade,
King of Clubs, but trumped out most, just like the ace of spades.
He stood knee-deep in troubled waters, looked adversity in the face,
Often looked upon as a foreign man, an alien from outer space.

But he kept on moving,
Went hard in the paint, even when his toes got stomped.
His will assuring him, he can if he can't,
Parlayed disasters into triumphs.

The odds stacked high, kept the prize in his eye,
Even turbulent storms couldn't shake him.
If it's all a dream, which it may very well be,
Please do not bother to wake him.

Known As a Fighter

In the zone on the throne,
My badge of honor is encrusted;
Never far away from home,
Always revered and ever-trusted.

Always discreet in defeat,
But not pomp in triumph.
There is no thing in these streets,
That I am quick to run from.

Though, my life is a mess,
I am doing my best.
To ease pain and distress,
From behind the "S" on my chest.

The final chapter to my novel,
And a pause to my striving.
A lie, before the end of this stanza,
Once again, I'll be writing.

A stinger that will linger,
Like in the ass of a bumble bee.
A singer for the moving finger,
Through life and death, I am a humble bee.

I have had the clout before,
So I don't get excited.
Any and all comers are welcome,
Matter of fact, sometimes, invited.

With a pen as a gun,
And words as my ammunition.
I suggest that you do your best,
And play your position.

No blunder or wonder of my giving and giving,
My best foot forward, in this world, whether surviving or living.
The compassion of a deacon, and fearless mind of a rider,
Not only a survivor, I'm also known as a fighter.

My soul is unconquerable, and it is ever-redeeming;
There's a light shining on me, and it's constantly beaming.
Like a well-battered boxer, or a stressed out coach,
With diligence as my road map—fortitude, my approach.

Outstretched hands to the heavens, mine most certainly are;
And that is, of course, how I've made it thus far.
It's assurance when I tell you that it is a "done dada,"
Defiance—no reliance, on Gucci or Prada.

To the bottom, I am common; I so often haunt,
The unpopular stores, to get what no one else wants.
I say the things that only a foolish man would,
And clothes do not make me; I help to make them look good.

Money is nice, but it was never my focus;
The tax collectors have tried, but even they have not broke us.
Spoken of in certain circles as a hell of a target to hit,
Modesty has been my key, so I deny every bit.

Bragging is not an option, and boasting is a no no,
For, it is not in the sound at all; but instead, it is in the show.
Every fight, every battle, recognized by the ferocity of a tiger,
Nothing else suffices when, to the world, you're known as a fighter.

A single square in a pack, like a box of cigarettes,
Self-proclaimed underdog, in life, so why not in the bets?
My visions are wider, and my horizons are clear;
I will not repeat it, so it is imperative that you hear.

Straight-on strategist, believe in me; battleships soon will be sunk;
Only knowing can quench my thirst, and I'm trying to get drunk.
The lessons I've learned have been a trial by fire,
I will die for respect; don't attempt to make me a liar.

With "back track" on the shelf and "retreat" laying still,
Please, make no mistake; I can fight and I will.
Thirty second timeout! I do not need a rest;
Just time for my team to get air—a second wind in their breasts.

A tactic rejuvenation, like a wartime revival,
Only such would be fitting in the life of a rider.
Fierce protector of my woman, my child, and my brethren,
Sex serves as many things, just not as a weapon.

A "hide and seek" loser, never been much of a hider,
Harder to back down than lose, when you are known as a fighter.

Merit Badge

Please forgive the intrusion,
And pardon the interruption.
But this tale of mine,
Really needs no introduction.

You can call me Mr. Modest;
I've never been a whore for glory.
It's never safe to believe all you hear,
But there is truth to my story.

Not many people could have endured;
They would rather have just up and died.
But I wouldn't have learned to walk,
If I hadn't, first, fell when I tried.

I don't have the answers,
But will fill you in on what I know.
I dot my I's and cross my T's,
To have a circle of friends each and everywhere I go.

The echoes are bellowing,
To all those listening in the night.
Lightning flames the name,
While it's glistening in the lights.

Mental mirages enticed my mind,
But didn't contribute to my hubris.
A dream is a dream until you write it on paper,
Then, it becomes a "to do" list.

For many, the path to success,
Is a hard pill to swallow.
But in order to be strong enough to lead,
You have to be humble enough to follow.

Be calm and the world wants to see you talked about,
As reward for being humble.
Be careful in being talked about,
Because, then, the world wants to see you humbled.

There never was a need for me, to step on backs to help my gain;
I have made it in this game, because I have stayed within my lane.
To the bonds of friendship, I am truly promiscuous;
Relating to many like in Leviticus, I'm so meticulous, it is ridiculous.

And though I run the risk, of simply risking running,
I am finding that all my trying, is relying on my cunning.
With a head full of steam, and a mouth full of manners,
My eyes focus on team, with our goal as the planner.

It is with great pride that I,
Proclaim to be one of the city's favorite sons.
I am known, true,
But not too known and not known to make the machine run.

In my quest for best, my test has had traps that couldn't harm me,
A brave and noble soldier, in the mighty king's army.
For a chance to embrace life, I was very very ready;
I wanted it just like, pilgrims want water in the Serengeti.

I never was the guy, to pursue the furs and the minks,
But craved stoic expression, like the unchanging Sphinx.
Far from sedentary sitting, like a battery's corrosion,
Not quite a night at the opera, or a gospel explosion.

But my persona introduces clarity, with every rumbling word;
It shakes the ground with its presence, like it was a rumbling herd.

Only Me

I'm gonna look over the scene and scan through the crowd;
I have no need to mug mean, or too be really loud.
When I approach from the rear, and I head to the front,
You might think I've been smoking, but you don't smell a blunt.

Looking like a shark in the dark, I favor a cub in the light;
Don't let the baby face fool you; I possess the heart to fight.
I'm a lion at heart and, yet, a kicker in stature;
While da Vinci in art, I am a soldier, in battle.

Maybe aggressive, in speech, but I'm not evil with people;
Whenever I'm talking, I'm teaching; and I am my brother's keeper.
There are no shackles or chains, that could bound down my feet;
I don't bite my tongue, and I won't grit my teeth.

There's no easy way that you can make me upset;
But when I get mad, it's best to call in the bets.
Disrespect my home; I promise, I'm gonna defend it;
If there's victory to win, and I am in it, I'll win it.

(I feel…)

It's the warmth of my heart that gives off a glow;
And an unchanging attitude, that everyone knows.
It's the truth that you know, after everything that I've told you,
From the chilled, cool demeanor, while I keep my composure.

Anyone that knows me, probably should've told you,
That I live like a man, but I would die like a soldier.
Very hard to explain, so I'll try to help you to see,
Only a man, until I die, and a man is only me.

There are some things, in this life, that some might not understand;
But I can peep through muddy water, and I can spot the dry land.
One important thing, in life, that my sight has let me see,
Is how much I need my people, and what my queen means, to me.

Object of my affection, and true co-ruler of my kingdom,
She's central focus of my protection, and a pearl to all my wisdom.
Always down from the jump, she's not in it for cheddar,
Instead, always says, "It's okay, and I'm sure it will get better."

(It's obvious…)

The wind beneath my wings, she's always pushing me higher;
So I'd give my life for her, and I could never fight her.
The comfort of her love, it seems to make me go blind;
It's her warm pumping heart, beating close, next to mine.

She is one of the greatest treasures, any hunter could ever find;
The love that I have found for her, could stand the tests of time.
Behind me, making me the best man I can be,
She knows I am a man, and a man is only me.

In my life, there aren't a lot of people who understand me;
Those that do, I call my folks, whether kinship or blood family.
They are my very support—my base, foundation, and backing;
From them, I draw strength; they help me wherever I'm lacking.

They have my love and loyalty; my trust won't let me doubt them;
Any good I am is because of them; I would be nothing without them.
I wouldn't waste time, take last dimes, or food out of their mouths;
I know when I am down and out, they always help a brother out.

(That's why…)

They are giving me wisdom, every day, as I grow older,
Like a cut man in my corner, or angels on my shoulders.
They are my people—some blood; we intertwine like kud;
They share my unyielding loyalty, and my undying love.

Like the stitch of my shirt, or sharp crease in my slacks,
They are the will in my power; they are the bones in my back.
Always doing best, they try to help me to see,
That I am always a man, and a man is only me.

In concluding the discussion, there is but one person left;
No one completes a man, unless it's the man, himself.
Taking the knocks and the shocks, as well as bumps and the bruises,
He always realizes decisions, whether he accepts or refuses.

Never raises hands to a woman, or selfishly watches a child cry,
Keep his head loose on a swivel, but face lifted to the sky.
Remembering where he came from, need to represent it for home,
Know, to the core, no one lives this life, all alone.

(It's clear...)

I'm the "Don of the family," and chip off the old block;
I am on a roll, now, and I've come too far to stop.
From my quest for more knowledge—the path that I have trod,
It's my respect for the ladies, and my strong faith in God.

The mistakes that I've made, you need to understand,
I am NOTHING SPECIAL; I am but a man.
My haste in priority, how I keep stern control,
After God, I rule my fate and I umpire my soul.

It's the depth of my soul, and the cool of my mood;
It's my natural aggression, and my pure attitude.
From the crown of my head, to the soles of my feet,
It's the only me, every day, born to die belief.

Self-proclaimed as the truth, realest you'll ever meet,
I am the blaring trumpet, that won't ever sound "retreat."
Unbelievable vision, it is my space age plan;
A man is all I can be, 'cause I am just a man.

The Utility Man

You said that you missed me, when you were out there on the block;
I want to own where you stand, so I am off punching the clock.
Dirty dealings and raw deals, really just do not move me,
Though I'm steadily chasing cheese, like my name were Ratatouille.

One day, I will leave this life; I'll ascend from here to Heaven;
Though not a prophet, I prophesy I'll, some day, live as a legend.
I play by my own rules—to the system, sometimes, defiant;
Though game plan not yet defined, I'm destined to be a giant.

In a class of my own, other jokers do not deserve a mention;
Believe, I am the utility man; plainly put, I have no competition.
I'm thinking of the next move, while you slumber and sleep;
And I tend to do more by noon, than you will try to do in a week.

Usually humble when making plays, my deeds outweigh my talk;
It is by my sight I see, but it's by my faith that I walk.
Since action stands as evidence, there is no dismissing;
My passion is unrelenting; otherwise, I would be conflicting.

To my drive, that shows I'm alive; I swear I'll always give my all;
My lifeline will be busy, until the Lord decides to call.
And when it is time to rest, I know He reserved a seat for me;
When I can speak no more, may the work I've done speak for me.

Fast Track to Success

My hopes motivate me to get it all in;
Vision helps me to think larger.
Dedicated to dreams, refusing to give up,
Like my name was Stix from "Sparkle."

There seems to be an agenda,
And, though, the big plan is to foil me.
I am used to all the turmoil;
It is perseverance that spoils me.

I hurdled over the hurdle's stand;
The obstacles came and they went.
I pushed weight up with calloused hands;
I split my vaulting stick.

Going hard in every realm,
Always, until there was nothing left.
Although a formidable competitor,
Even I could not beat myself.

Straight fingers and crooked grins,
Will never get in the way.
From known foes to impostor friends,
In spite of what all of them say.

Vigilant foe to failure,
And malicious, in regards to mess.
Familiar to finding,
The fastest track to the slowest success.

The Final Bell

Haven't always been on,
But have never been a scrub.
Acknowledge respect by the daps,
And the love by the hugs.

The Dimetap of fast talk,
On the throne but uncrowned.
With a walk to match the talk,
Known to slow that ass down.

I stay as cool as a fan;
Never keep a beef about me.
You can check my record in the classroom;
You can ask the streets about me.

(Just think…)

Who knew that that humble little boy from around Cherry Drive,
With passion in his speech and ambition in his eyes.
Would be able to find his own way, build castles of his own,
That he who had been so weak, would grow to be so strong.

At one time, in any battle, it was unconceivable that he win it;
Now, he is welcome to the world and anything that he finds in it.
I'm sure I surprised a lot of folks, with the things I chose to explore,
When there was no way, I made my mind to go Bogart the door.

Throwing caution to the wind, jumping in legs back and head first,
With an incurable longing and a real insatiable thirst.
Doing things the way I see fit, I've been compared to a rebel,
The world complains very seldom; I grew a boulder from a pebble.

(Do the research…)

When you hear the lion roaring, better believe the hunter's coming;
I have proved that it is not a crime, to hit the new ground running.
Those standing in my path, need to see what's left in my tracks;
If you do not intend to get trampled, I suggest that you step back.

As far as I'm concerned, this world that I live is partly mine,
The things it can produce for me, and everything within its confines.
I know the key to my successes, answers to all obstacles overcome,
Common denominators in all of this, is God and where I am from.

The Lord's grace and mercy, keeps me from day to day;
My mother and father were the ones, who taught me to pray.
Daddy did his duty, to ensure I end up as I am,
As steadfast as the old tortoise, and humble as the little lamb.

(Listen to me…)

My back's really aching; and my eyes are steadily throbbing;
That is why I am scratching, and biting, and crawling.
My hands are hardening, and my feet getting tender;
In the bout's final seconds, I am resisting surrender.

While my opponent's trainers, reduce the swell of his eyes,
My very own have the task, of helping me to survive.

Atlas of the World

Always giving back,
With every part I get.
And the world could care less,
Don't appreciate it a bit.

No insincere encounters;
Never vehement in dealings.
But strictly with the purpose,
Of building up and healing.

Who cares about my sadness,
Behind the mask that I've been wearing?
Who cares about my frowns,
When pain gets overbearing?

(That's Why…)

I take sand in my hand,
And get a better handle.
Reach down to my ankles,
And I tighten up my sandals.

Pressure nor imbalance,
Will ever succeed to defeat me.
I kick away the rocks,
In order to get my feet beneath me.

Though, I don't receive the privilege,
Or the pomp march of the band.
I hoist the globe to my shoulders,
I can squat or I can stand.

Guaranteed excitement,
Through blatant hating eyes,
Like embers of blazing fires,
In the night, still I rise.

Though stomped and snuffed, beyond roughed up,
For me, even epic storms are not strong enough.
No crying or running, like a child or woman,
I just gain my composure, and I keep on coming.

(Notice…)

Through the storm and the rain,
No one can fathom my strain.
A life forced to abnegation,
Saturated with pain.

While others still search,
Hardily, to find the road.
I have learned that I am,
Forced to carry the load.

Feed like The Salvation,
If it means my deprivation.
And every time I do it all,
No complaints or hesitation.

Is acquittal too much to ask?
An end to this bland dismay?
It is not even behind my back;
It's the middle finger to my face.

Growing wiser and bolder, every day I grow older,
Knelt down to the ground, rose with the world on my shoulders.

Hey Reader,

I am glad that you have joined me, again. I cannot say it enough; your support means the world to me! As has been my style, I write about anything. I just need a subject. Lol. I love it. What I hope that you got from this project is that life is full of experiences. Some experiences are good, while others are bad. What they both have in common is that we can learn from any and all experiences—be it our own or those of others. Never discount that. Not every experience will be something to write home about. New cars are great. Closings on homes are to be celebrated. I won't deny that. Can you find the opportunity in the little things? Can you find inspiration in the little guy? Can you find strength in the helpless and hope in the hopeless? 1 Corinthians 1:27 tells us that, "God hath chosen the foolish things of the world to confound the wise; and God hath chosen the weak things of the world to confound the things which are mighty." As you go forward, I challenge you to change your thinking. Don't count out the runt of the litter. Thank you for reading. Be blessed and Godspeed.

-HJ

www.ingramcontent.com/pod-product-compliance
Lightning Source LLC
Chambersburg PA
CBHW051727040426
42447CB00008B/1005